Discover Christmas

by Victoria Marcos

© 2012 by Victoria Marcos
Hardcover ISBN: 978-1-5324-3712-0
Paperback ISBN: 978-1-62395-476-5   -   EPUB ISBN: 978-1-62395-477-2
Images licensed from Fotolia.com
First Edition
Published in the United States by Xist Publishing
www.xistpublishing.com
Xist Publishing

xist Publishing

It's Christmas time!

Some kids go to the Christmas tree lot to pick out a Christmas tree. There are many trees to choose from - tall, short, narrow and wide. When they find the perfect tree they tie it to the roof of their car, take it home and decorate it.

This tree is being decorated with red ornaments and bows. Long strands of gold beads are placed around the tree on the branches. You can make your own ornaments that would make your Christmas tree very special!

6

The Christmas tree is lit up with a long strand of lights that are placed around the tree and hidden in the branches. The more lights you put on the tree the better you can
see the ornaments!

See how well the Christmas tree lights light up all the ornaments? It's so bright that you don't need to turn on any lights to see the stockings hung on the mantel.

Everyone in the family hangs a stocking on the mantel. Stockings are filled with toys, candy and books. A long time ago, people used to hang their socks on the mantel to dry. This is how the tradition of hanging stockings on the mantel began.

The Christmas tree is surrounded by lots of beautifully wrapped presents. Everyone's presents have a card that has their name on it. Which one is your present?

The toy train travels around and around the Christmas tree. It's fun to pretend the train is filled with presents that it drops off to children all over the world. What is the train going to drop off at your house?

You can use branches from a Christmas tree and berries from a holly bush to make a Christmas wreath to hang on the front door. It will help get you in the holiday spirit!

Some kids make Christmas cards for their relatives and friends. They write a Christmas greeting inside and sign their names. They mail them early to make sure they arrive before Christmas day.

Decorating a gingerbread house is a tradition during the Christmas season. You can use frosting for the icicles and gummy candies for bricks. A cotton ball pulled apart looks like smoke coming out of the chimney. It almost looks too good to eat!

When we see candy canes we think of Christmas. Not only do they taste good, but they can be used as ornaments on a Christmas tree!

A snow globe is made of glass and has water inside. You can make it snow on the children inside by shaking the globe. It looks like a toy, but it's not. You need to be careful not to drop it because it may break.

These toy soldiers are characters from the ballet "The Nutcracker." The Nutcracker is most popular during the Christmas season. These soldiers are toys and are also used as Christmas decorations.

This stained glass window tells the story of Nativity. The three wise men brought gifts to Jesus when he was born on Christmas day. Can you see the star?

The family dog gets in the Christmas spirit by wearing a Santa hat. He wears his hat when he poses with his family in their Christmas pictures. Isn't he cute?

This reindeer has very big antlers. Male reindeer have much bigger antlers than female. Legend has it that reindeer pull Santa's sleigh. Have you ever seen a reindeer?

One fun thing to do during Christmas break is to make a snowman. Can you name all the things you'll need to make snow into a man? Don't forget to wear your jacket, gloves and boots. It's cold outside!

This girl is telling Santa what she wants for Christmas. Santa asked her if she's been naughty or nice. It looks as though she's been nice because Santa is smiling.

Santa delivers presents in a big red bag on Christmas morning. He makes lots of children very happy! What did you ask for this year?

Before you go to bed on Christmas Eve, leave a plate of cookies and a glass of milk for Santa by the fireplace. Don't forget his reindeer.
They love carrots!

Merry Christmas!

www.ingramcontent.com/pod-product-compliance
Lightning Source LLC
Chambersburg PA
CBHW040417110426
42813CB00013B/2686